My Dad Is In Jail

Written By: Amber M. Ryan

Illustrated By: Heather Torres

Copyright © 2013 RT Books
ISBN-13: 978-0615897561
ISBN-10: 0615897568

Printed by CreateSpace
eStore address https://www.createspace.com/4445838
Available from Amazon.com, CreateSpace.com, and Kindle

All rights reserved.

My dad went to jail and it makes me cry. I miss him a lot and I don't understand why.

Why did he do it? Why did he leave?

How long until he comes home? Make him hurry, please!

Sometimes he calls.

Sometimes he writes.

I miss him tucking me in at night.

I missed him at Christmas and Easter, too.

I missed him last week when we went to the zoo.

He promised he would coach my baseball team.

And ride the rollercoaster that makes us scream.

He missed my recital and he missed my school play.

My whole life has changed since my dad went away.

My mom says it's ok to cry when I'm sad.

And sometimes when I'm mad, I'm really just sad.

My Nana says it's normal to feel like I am missing a part. My dad and I are close. He has stolen my heart.

There's a boy in my class and his dad's in jail too. He understands why I sometimes feel blue.

My dad will be happy to know I learned new spelling words this week.

I can't wait to tell him I tried snails to eat!

I'm making good grades and learning a ton.

Not only am I learning, I am also having fun!

I'm counting the days until I see my dad again.

I hope he learns a lesson from where he has been.

Until that day comes, I promise to keep, all the lessons he taught me tucked away nice and neat.